RUM
and
BACCY

True Tales of a Sailor in the 1960s and 70s

Bernie Howard

Bright Pen

Visit us online at www.authorsonline.co.uk

A Bright Pen Book

Copyright © B J Howard 2014

Cover design by B J Howard ©

All rights reserved. No part of this publication may be reproduced, stored in a retrieval system, or transmitted in any form or by any means, electronic, mechanical, photocopy, recording or otherwise, without prior written permission of the copyright owner. Nor can it be circulated in any form of binding or cover other than that in which it is published and without similar condition including this condition being imposed on a subsequent purchaser.

British Library Cataloguing Publication Data.
A catalogue record for this book is available from the British Library

ISBN 978-0-7552-1650-5

Authors OnLine Ltd
19 The Cinques
Gamlingay, Sandy
Bedfordshire SG19 3NU
England

www.authorsonline.co.uk

Introduction

In the years since leaving the sea there have been many times whilst in conversation that I have had said to me that I should write a book.

Some of the tales I've written about are over forty years old and it has been great for me to recall memories of people, places and times of my life at sea in the Royal and Merchant Navy in the nineteen sixties and seventies.

I would like to thank the people who prompted me to write this and especially my good friend Allan Child who in so doing has brought about fond memories of times that shouldn't be forgotten.

Contents

My Favourite Poem

Good Lord above send down a dove
With wings as sharp as razors
To cut the throats
Of them there blokes
Who sell bad beer to sailors.

Definition of a Dance

Naval encounter without the loss of seamen.

Chapter 1 – Ganges

I was always going to sea when I left school, God knows why, as there had never been a sailor in my family, and the only ships I'd ever seen were rowing boats at Hunstanton. In those days, prospective employers came to your school to head hunt, so when someone came from the Merchant Navy I went along and listened. Everything sounded great until the bit where you had to pay for uniform and training, and although not much, I did not think that my father's wage would cover the halfpence of tar they cost. It was the same thing with the Fishing Fleet, and then along came the Royal Navy. Not only was there nothing to pay but you got paid. I was sold.

I had my medical in London on my fifteenth birthday having previously passed the entrance exams, so in the early summer of 1962 I was off. My father took me to Swaffham Station and as the Norwich train pulled in he told me, as he pushed me onto the train, that I didn't have to go if I didn't want to, placed half a crown in my hand and shut the door.

On arrival at Norwich I made the short walk to the Recruiting Office on Prince of Wales Road, where the rest of the Norfolk conscripts were waiting. A burly petty officer, who seemed like he'd had a tot too many, told us he hated Geordies and warned us to look out for them. He gave us the Queen's shilling and sent us back to the station to catch the Ipswich train where we began our journey to HMS Ganges.

Ganges was a boy's training establishment at Shotley which was just a few miles from Ipswich; being the size of a small town it housed two thousand two hundred boys and a few hundred ship's company. By looking over the water you could see the ports of Harwich and Felixstowe.

On arriving at Ipswich we were met by lads not much older than us but in uniform, and petty officers who told us to wait together until the next train came in, then we would be taken by lorry to a place called the Annex.

The next train pulled in and out jumped what looked like a Borstal contingent. These lads looked bigger than us; all dressed in "TeddyBoy" suits or leather jackets and jeans, D. A. haircuts, sideburns, they looked tough and a voice behind me said, "Jocks and Geordies". So this was a Geordie, obviously a Jock's friend. Now us lads from Norfolk were mainly in school uniform, some even in short trousers, so we felt very intimidated.

We were now bundled into wagons with R.N. painted on the doors. A few miles up the road we passed HMS Ganges and pulled up at our destination – the Annex.

For the next six weeks we were prepared for life at Ganges, kitted out with uniforms, work clothes, sports kit and anything else we needed. We said goodbye to our civilian clothes and the next thing was hair cuts. So it was off for a quick visit to Shotley, the Ganges barber. Shotley could scalp a boy in seconds flat, so this visit didn't take long. Now wearing the same clothes and with bald heads, we all looked the same, and the only way we could tell a Geordie or Jock from the rest was by not having a clue what they were saying. It wasn't long, however, that we all picked up bits of each other's lingo, dropped certain bits, and somehow formed our own language.

The Annexe was horrific – up at half past five in the morning for a freezing shower, double everywhere (run), no talking, no smiling, nothing on bread, no sugar, no toilet doors, no TV or radio, and after having been screamed at 'til seven o'clock in the evening, we retired to bed. Here we had to keep complete silence, but after only a few minutes some unfortunate would start crying or sneeze or a moth would fart. Screaming would start up again. Up we'd get, put all of our newly gained kit into our kit bags, go out to the Parade Ground with kit bags on our shoulders, and we'd run round and round until someone collapsed. I've done this in the pouring rain in pyjamas.

After a couple of weeks we had to march into Ganges to climb the mast. Our instruction for this was that it's 142 feet high and has a net a dozen feet from the ground. Should you fall from halfway up, apparently you'd bounce off the net and go through the Post Office roof. If, however, you were near to the top, the net would make you into chips. There were P.T.I's (physical training instructors) at different footage on the mast, which we thought were to help if you were in any difficulty; however, their purpose was, should you freeze in fear as many did, to scurry above the unfortunates and jam on their hands. Anyway, it must have worked because we all passed without anyone being chipped.

Being in the Navy you had to be able to swim and should you not pass the given test, you became a backward swimmer and had to go to the swimming pool at six o'clock in the morning every day until passing. First of all, you had to put on freezing cold, soaking wet overalls and then, lined up around the deep end, you'd get pushed in one by one. Then sink or swim. If you swam to the side – great, if you sank they'd hook you out with poles then, apparently to teach you quicker, you'd get pushed off the top board. This worked for me and I passed in three days.

After six weeks in the Annexe we marched with our kitbags on our shoulders to Ganges itself where Rodney 16 Mess was to be my home for the next forty-six weeks. Our new home had to be kept immaculate; the bins and floors were literally like mirrors and in any spare time we were kept busy polishing with boot brushes. Our mess was on Long

Covered Way which was like a road covered with mess decks either side. I can imagine it about a quarter of a mile long. This also had to be immaculate and was kept so mainly by misfortunates with toothbrushes scrubbing away for hours on end and being punished for talking or having spots or some other crime.

Our days were now kept busy by school, instruction, drill, sport, seamanship, rowing, kit maintenance, numerous inspections including arseholes and foreskins. This I can't make out to this day. About once a week we had to stand in pyjamas at the end of our beds with kit laid out for inspection. As the Officer and Chief Petty Officer passed you dropped your pyjama bottoms, pulled back your foreskins, turned around and opened your cheeks. Our embarrassment must have been their pleasure.

Ganges used to hold a cinema in the gym. I think it was on a Wednesday and films were advertised on the side of the Parade Ground. The cost was around sixpence, a fortune to those of us who only earned fifteen shillings a week – seventy-five pence in today's money. After being in Ganges for about six weeks we were told we could go to the cinema.

A friend and I queued up in the rain for two hours to see a Dean Martin and Jerry Lewis comedy. On paying, we sat on one of the many forms laid out for the show. The Chiefs and Petty Officers were at the back on more comfortable chairs all chatting away whilst us boys had to keep complete silence. The film had only been going for a few minutes when Jerry Lewis started his antics and a boy two rows back from us started to giggle. A petty officer stormed down and kicked six rows of us out. Apparently you mustn't laugh at a funny film.

There were many types of punishment at Ganges, the most severe being cuts. Cuts was a form of the birch and I was to taste this very painful ordeal. I had been on weekend leave to Swaffham where, at a Youth Club dance, in a fight I injured a lad from Kings Lynn, and got arrested. The next day I was escorted back to Ganges where I was put on Captain's Report and awarded six cuts. To receive your cuts you had on your works trousers inside out. This enabled you to lean over the bench, a patrolman to pull on one pocket one side and another patrolman to pull on the other. A third patrolman who was about twenty stone had the cane and delivered the strokes. After each stroke your ass was inspected to make sure you'd been cut and that the strokes didn't cross. It was impossible to lay on your back or sit down in Instructions for a few weeks after this. Later, upon leaving the Royal Navy, the Master of Arms who oversaw this took a pub in Swaffham called the White Lion on Station Street and he became a very good friend of mine. Tony Meredith was his name and I had great respect for him.

After a year you left Ganges a "TROG" which you'd be 'til the day you die. TROG quite simply means Trained Rating Of Ganges. Ganges had been very tough and even cruel, but for me if helped me to deal with life afterwards, facing as you do many a tricky situation.

Junior Mess – HMS Ganges

Chapter 2 – Walter Raleigh

My first draft on leaving HMS Ganges was to HMS Raleigh, in Torpoint, Devon, just over from Plymouth, which was an engineering training base for those that were older than us, most being eighteen to about twenty-four. Also at HMS Raleigh was a Wrens' training section. The idea for us being there was a bit more training whilst waiting for a ship. We had all been looking forward to meeting the Wrens for a bit of female company after being with two thousand two hundred boys for the past year. As it turned out, the Wrens were unavailable. There was a bridge over to their quarters which was guarded twenty- four hours a day. It was strongly rumoured that two ratings had broken in a few years previously and had been wanked to death. This did not stop the plans at tea breaks on how to break in. The most popular methods were tunnelling or making friends with a para. One thing about the Wrens which I couldn't get my head around was when it was the Wrens' time of the month they had to walk instead of march. The unfortunates would either walk ahead or behind the marching squad which told all and sundry of their predicament. This led to a lot of catcalls and remarks from simple sailors.

HMS Raleigh had a mascot which was a very badly behaved goat called Walter. Whilst I was on one duty watch, I had the pleasure of cleaning out Walter's stable and feeding him, but the best part was still to come. Walter also drew his fag rations – twenty a day to be fed after his meal. He wasn't so lucky with me but I gave him ten and enjoyed the other half of the dessert myself. It was great to see Walter on parade on special occasions. He would be dressed in his mascot colours and some unfortunate would have him on a lead but he'd go berserk and was uncontrollable.

Another memory of HMS Raleigh was a boxing tournament which I entered. In this tournament, if successful, you would have three fights in a day. In my first bout I stopped my opponent in the second round: in the second fight I got a bye for some reason, and in the final I was beaten up by a very muscular Nigerian. I collected my Runner's Up prize from a Wren Officer. This was a bit of cloth with writing on it. When entering the Changing Room, I pushed this into my pocket to look at later on my own as my eyes were sore and swollen. After showering and changing I went for a few drinks and forgot all about my prize until the next day when I discovered that, for being runner up in the finals, I'd won a bit of navy cloth which somebody had roughly sewn "Boxing" across. Years later I trained amateur boxers who, on their very first fight after losing, would get a statue or a cup.

It was also whilst at HMS Raleigh that I got my first tattoo and earring. Earrings were allowed but frowned upon and on morning parade a chief petty officer noticed how a few of us were sporting our new purchases. "Gypsies, homosexuals and thieves wear earrings and as the Royal Navy enlist none of these, get them out you travelling thieving queers." In my first ship I put my earring back and have worn one since.

The tattoos we scarred our bodies with were absolutely terrible. I can't believe that after getting one we were daft enough to go back every pay day for more. Professor Zeta was the name of the tattooist. He was fat and unkempt and always proud to show you his nipples, with rings in. This was unheard of at the time. The first tattoo I got was of a Japanese sailor girl with Japan spelt out underneath. The sailor girl was nothing but a smudge and luckily I've been to Japan a few times since. I then got the signs for playing cards but he managed to put the spade upside down. These were followed by a snake's head that looked like a doberman and a butterfly which could have been anything. Never mind. I was now ready and waiting for my first ship.

Chapter 3 – Pompey

Portsmouth in the sixties and seventies was one big playground for sailors. There were enough pubs on every street for a pub crawl and enough sailors to fill every pub.

One of my favourites was the Alderman – it was always full of unforgettable characters. "Gypsy Pete" was a gay who would mince in and sit on a high stool at the bar so he could see himself in the bar mirror. After getting his first pint he'd start to preen himself in the mirror, combing his hair and pouting his lips. This would continue for a few pints when he would start to fall out with himself, ending up in a full-blown argument where he would be calling his reflection every expletive under the sun. "Big Silve" was another regular never to be forgotten. Silve was a large lady of the night or in her case a lady of twenty-four hours. Not a person to mess with as she could and would fight like a man. Apparently she had tattoos at the top of both of her legs – one saying, "Sailors Rest" and the other one saying, "Pay Before You Enter". I was enjoying a drink one summer dinner time when, apart from sailors, there were a lot of holidaymakers in the pub. As Silve walked in she shouted across to me saying, "Get us a pint of scrumps love, I'm just going for a shit." No, Silve wasn't the type to take home and meet mum but she had a heart of gold.

Just down from Unicorn Dockyard gates there were two very cheap eating establishments which also had reasonably priced rooms to rent. They were both run for the Navy. Aggie Weston's was one and the Trafalgar Club was the other. Although the prices were as cheap as you'd get, me and a mate Nicky Whelan devised a plan where we ate for free and no queuing, as after the pubs had shut these were very popular establishments. What we'd do was go straight to the front of the queue and grab a clean plate and cutlery, and then we'd head for the tables that had been vacated but not yet cleared away. We would then pile our plates with leftovers – half a sausage from here, a leftover yolk from another; chips and beans were in abundance and bread was always available. Whelan even got fussy and started to go for just what was still warm. Sometimes we'd really go to town and grab leftover half- eaten sweets as well. This really was fine dining.

Every now and again I'd have a night out at the dog track. Portsmouth Dog Track only had five dogs in each race and I always bet traps two and five in a forecast. This meant you had to get first and second to win. One night I won on quite a few occasions and bagged a total of £36, which was the equivalent of more than a month's pay. At the track here was also a casino, so with my new wealth I thought I'd wager some of it on blackjack and become richer. In the casino I sat down at the blackjack table and ordered a fine cigar and a double scotch. The dealer was a young girl who was very well gifted in the bosom department. For the moment I felt like a king. Unfortunately, half an hour later I had to walk back to my ship in the rain with not a penny left. Easy come, easy go.

On Navy Days, Portsmouth would be packed with sightseers, sailors, parents, girlfriends and anyone with a following of the Navy. Ships and shore establishments were packed with visitors – pubs and restaurants were extremely busy. I went ashore with a good mate of mine from East Dereham at dinner time; our first call was the very first pub straight over the road from the Main Dockyard gate. For whatever reason I can't remember I got into a fight at the bar, which escalated into a three- pub free for all. There must have been a hundred involved. Police and Naval Patrol arrived but instead of arresting people, it seemed they wanted some fun or had had a bad day, because they joined in as well. When reinforcements arrived, in the words of John Wayne, "We got the hell out of there," and were saved from being arrested.

Portsmouth was also a great place for live entertainment. I went to see the Rolling Stones in the Guildhall. I was waiting outside when they arrived and Mick Jagger minced past with a white poodle and the crowd went wild. The Savoy Dance Hall in Southsea used to book Manfred Mann and I saw them on a few occasions. Also at the Mecca I went to see Eric Burdon and the Animals, who were brilliant.

Chapter 4 – Rum alias Grog or The Tot

As ratings, from the age of twenty you became entitled to the tot, or if you didn't want it, you became T and received threepence a day. Our rum was mixed as to one part rum to two parts water and this made up a tumbler full. Chiefs and petty officers had theirs neat. The reason ours had to be drunk as mixed with water was so you couldn't bottle and keep.

The strength of the rum was this: one tot and you would become gibberish and have the ability to eat any crap put before you; two tots you were pissed, three legless, four or five could kill you.

There was also a lot of strict protocol. Rum was collected in a fanny which was a metal urn and dished out by one rating with another rating ticking off as you collected. When you got your rum you gave each of these a wet, which was about a teaspoonful. The next amount given for a favour was a sip which was about a tablespoonful followed by a gulp which was about two tablespoonfuls. God help anyone who took a sip instead of a wet or a gulp. Half tots were sometimes given which was half a glass. These were only given for really big favours.

Rum came up at around twelve o'clock dinner time. A rum station was set up where a large open- topped barrel would be placed to top up with a wooden keg of rum and the appropriate water. There would be an officer in charge of this delicate procedure.

In HMS Zulu this station was set up by a water cooler at the top of our messdeck ladder. Now when all the messdecks had collected their rum the remainder was disposed of down the water cooler, the pipe of which ran down into our messdeck. We soon found a join which we could undo and worked at it until it could be opened and closed easily. All we had to do now was get someone to hang about at the top of the ladder and give us the nod when the excess rum was being disposed of, then open the join, jug under and Hey Presto! This gave us roughly an extra third of a tot each and, on rare occasions, an extra tot. There was a snag, though, as the water cooler was a favourite place to throw up in after a night ashore, so we had to put up with bits of half- digested curries etc. but overall it was worth it.

The only time I was issued with neat rum (neaters) was when I was in field gun. As you had to keep one hundred per cent fit and so you didn't drink it, a blind eye was turned to bottling. On a weekend leave I took a bottle home to Swaffham for my mates to sample. In the lounge bar of the Kings Arms I shared out my ill-gotten gains. The next day my good friend Phil McCarthy, who could really drink, said to me, "I can't believe it. I came in at twenty past eight and was pissed by half past." That was the strength of the tot.

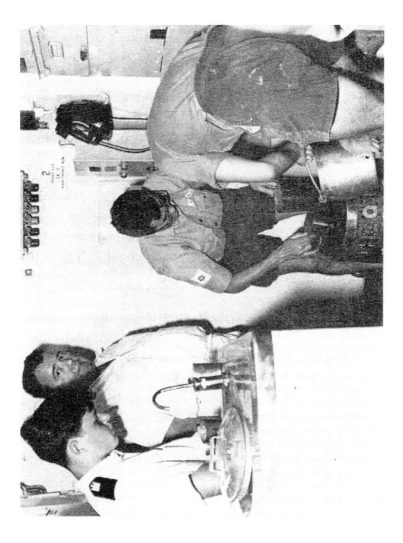

The offending water cooler with rum station

Chapter 5 – Gib

Gibraltar is a place I visited on many occasions. It would be nearly always the first port you'd stop off at on your way out and the last on the way home. There were numerous bars and duty free shops and a lot of sailors used Gib to buy their rabbits (presents) on the way home. This was very sensible as you could purchase most things here that you could buy in Singapore, Aden etc. for a similar price, and having on board only a small locker for your belongings, going on a rabbit run on your way home, you didn't have to keep your presents stored for long.

As far as the rock itself goes it was well worth a walk up. The Marines over a hundred years ago completed a fantastic engineering feat by digging tunnels and rooms out of the rock itself near the very top. These have been used for hospitals and shelter, and through carved- out windows are fantastic views of the Mediterranean. Halfway up are the monkeys (rock apes) whose purpose it seems is to rid sightseers of their belongings.

It was calling in at Gib on HMS Zulu where I had my worst encounter with the effects of rum. As we were only there for a few hours, four hours shore leave was given to each watch and the first call for leave was right on tot time, so a lot of us had seen Gib enough and swapped our four hours for the ones going ashore's rum. This meant two tots apiece plus what we'd got from splitting the pipe leading down from the water cooler as I mentioned before. After we'd drunk what was now the two tots apiece plus the cooler dregs, somebody brought out a bottle of neat rum, which he'd obtained from a petty officer for doing favours. We opened bottles of cane which was a strong spirit we'd obtained in South Africa. We were all by now very drunk and one lad had passed out and seemed to be changing colour. We tried to wake him up but to no avail. His complexion was by now greenish so in a drunken stupor somebody thought to make him sick and different techniques were tried but to no effect. After a bit longer a petty officer who was on rounds came down to the messdeck and in no time the ship's doc appeared. Our mate had now turned white and was pronounced dead. On sobering up hours later we were all feeling terrible with senses of guilt, but the truth was that it could have happened to any of us. Our Leading Hand who was in charge of us was ashore and although he had nothing to do with anything, on arrival back on board he was arrested for manslaughter. This had been a very sad day and lessons were learnt by all.

Chapter 6 – Alan T Smith

Whilst serving on HMS Ajax there was a lad from Kings Lynn, Norfolk called Alan T Smith. On arrival in Karachi Alan and I decided to go ashore. You had a choice of vehicle from where we were berthed; either a donkey or a selection of very old taxis. The latter was our choice. Driving into Karachi there was a large dark cloud which was moving in a strange way. As we got nearer there were thousands of people living in cardboard boxes and the strange dark cloud was flies hovering above. Deciding to get away from this we instructed our driver to take us to a nice place where we could get a drink. We were taken to what seemed like a drinking man's club. On entry we went to the bar where we could see that the prices were a bit above our means. Alan ordered a pint which was about ten times as dear as we were used to paying, so I bought a much cheaper coke. We went and sat on a very nice verandah where I unfortunately knocked over Alan's pint. Having to replace his, I thought if I've got to spend all this, I'll have one myself.

Now on board the ship, it had been of great interest to us what the T in Alan's name meant and although he was bugged incessantly about this he wouldn't tell. After a few more pints I got in my brain to find out the mystery of the T and kept pressurizing him, swearing secrecy that I'd tell no-one. Alan, after drumming into me the importance of keeping this secret until death, decided to tell me. Apparently he'd had a double-barrelled name which was Twait-Smith and his father had got so fed up with being called Twat Smith that he changed it to T Smith by deed poll.

This was information so brilliant that I shouldn't have been told and from the very next day Alan was known forever as Twat.

'Watchkeepers!!!'

'Watchkeepers'
Alan T Smith is on the far right

Chapter 7 – Subic Bay

Whilst serving on HMS Zulu we went to Subic Bay in the Philippines where we berthed in an American naval base. Just outside the base was a bridge and on here young boys of about five years old were selling baby ducklings. You got a dozen for a few shillings with the idea being that you threw them into the murky waters below, where waiting with open-mouthed anticipation were crocodiles. There weren't many hairy- assed matelots prepared to end the lives of these cute creatures in this way so they soon became pets.

Subic Bay was like being ashore in a live cowboy film. Outside every bar, sitting on rocking chairs were men with Stetsons and rifles across their laps. The entrances to the bars were swing doors and honky tonk music came from most of them. All were full of American sailors, prostitutes, the local drunks and degenerates and of course us with our pet ducks. They were by now so friendly that they would follow us to the next bar. The roads and paths were dirt and there were eating stalls everywhere serving mainly kebabs. The meat used was mainly monkey, or if like me you asked for chicken as no way did I want monkey, then chicken was promised – "Yes, yes Chicken", but you got monkey anyway.

In one of the bars where I can remember a midget on a donkey both pissed at the bar, I got into a fight with an American sailor who'd squashed one of my mates' ducks. Becoming the victor, I was ushered to the bar and given a large Bourbon by the bar owner. Apparently fights were appreciated as they went with the ambiance. On leaving, the barman shook my hand and said, "Hope to see you again". Later that evening I swapped uniforms with a young American and went back on board as a fully-fledged Yank. The next day there were baby ducklings everywhere and having no duck food, they were fed cheesy hammy eggies, roly polies, herrings or whatever else we could find. We obviously mashed this up but whether it was the diet or the lack of what mummy duck did, unfortunately one by one they died. We asked the ship's doc who said that apart from Aspros, there was nothing he could do. This was the same for us – headache Aspro, stomach ache Aspro, lost an arm Aspro and so after a few days they were all dead. Some had proper burials at sea and others were just flushed down the toilet, which I suppose if you think about it is the same thing.

A few years later, Subic Bay was flattened by a hurricane.

I recently looked up Subic Bay on YouTube and apart from the lack of ducks and shotguns, it still looks about the same. They also have an added bonus in that the American Navy is going back.

Chapter 8 – My Claim to Fame

One early afternoon in Hong Kong, me and my oppo Nutty Slack, feeling flush, thought we'd mix with the elite and have a drink in the Hong Kong Hilton.

We sat down and the waiter served our Tiger beers. The bar was empty apart from us and a fellow sitting on a seat by the window. On closer examination we could see that the fellow was none other than Jack Palance, a noted film star who had been an excellent middle weight boxer. I said to Nutty, "Let's go and have a drink with Jack", so we wandered across and were about to sit down and introduce ourselves when Jack said these immortal words, "You Limeys can fuck off – I'm no green Yank." Had we have become lifelong friends it would not have been as good as to have been told to "fuck off" by this screen legend.

Chapter 9 – Tales of Mombasa

Mombasa in Kenya was a brilliant place to visit for sailors in the nineteen sixties. Beer was cheap and good girls were cheap too. Well maybe not such good girls as for five shillings you could get a girl and a hotel room all night.

We had a leave centre called Silver Sands on Nyali Beach just down from the world famous Nyali Beach Hotel. This was out of bounds to us apart from high ranking officers and a night in the hotel cost them up to a thousand pounds. We were earning seven pounds a week. A few years ago I went back and now for a thousand pounds you get your flight, two weeks in the hotel, all the food you can eat plus a safari chucked in.

Nyali Beach is the best beach I've ever been on. It's like walking on fresh snow. The sea is completely safe to swim in because it's protected by a barrier reef. Our leave centre was great, and there was a bar and restaurant, library and skating rink, surrounded by huts which were where us and the mossies slept. Everything was run by the Church.

The first morning there I took a run along the beach which was deserted at that time. To my left was jungle, and to my right the sea. After about half a mile I heard what sounded like panting and yelping behind me. Hardly daring to look round, what I saw was a pack of wolves and they were after me. I picked up speed but to no avail and they were on me. I could see now that they were not wolves but alsatians but this did not make me feel any easier. Up they jumped but fortunately not to rip me apart but to lick me. They belonged to the leave centre and their job was to keep monkeys at bay. They had a continual battle and the dogs would kill the monkeys and indeed the monkeys would kill a dog. I had two stays at Silver Sands and one of the dogs kept with me all the time. I called him Chimp.

One evening whilst having a beer outside the skating rink there were about a dozen of us enjoying the evening cool down with the setting of the sun when a priest appeared. He was a stout fellow in his early thirties with a dog collar and an immaculate white shirt. At first, he went over to some other lads where he sat down and had a couple of beers. After about half an hour he excused himself and came over to us where he introduced himself as the Squadron Padre. Speaking to each in turn, it turned out he had a great knowledge of churches, as when it came to my turn, he said, "And where are you from my son?" On telling him "Swaffham, Norfolk", he replied, "Ah St Peter and St Paul's", which was correct. Being honourable sailors we decided to get him drunk so every time someone bought a round he was included. After quite a few beers and whiskies we realised that this would be no easy task as this man of the cloth could drink. A few of our lads were falling by the wayside, not able to keep up. The padre now became a singer with filthy jokes for the interludes. We even got a yard of ale but he soon polished this off and asked for another. Finally, on the closing of the bar a member of staff asked him, "Are you really a padre?" "Yes and these damn sailors have got me pissed again," he replied. I later found out he was a dishwasher on HMS Forth – what a character.

Whilst poking around in the library at Silver Sands I came across in a dusty leather- bound cover some original Punch sketches, which I took to the Reception thinking that they may have been of some value. Unfortunately I never heard of the outcome.

In Mombasa itself are two giant tusks which span a main road. These were given as a present by a certain Mr Campbell, a Scottish engineer who was out there building a dam. His wife was secretary to President Kenyatta and in later years lived in Swaffham. I sailed with his brother twice on Shell tankers in the Merchant Navy.

Around this area were a scattering of bars which we regularly used. When I first went in the bars I was amazed that men were going for a piss and coming back eating steak rolls. On going myself when the need arose, there right by the piss trough was a young man squatting on the floor over a pile of hot coals with a plate of uncovered raw meat beside. At least the rolls were in a bag. God only knows what the meat was. If you said beef it was beef, if you said hippo it was hippo. Anyway, after a few pints they were lovely.

One of the bars was called the Casablanca. It was bigger and offered more than most. It had cabaret with numerous different acts. I also wrestled there in a tag team. You'd earn ample to get pissed. It was here I met an old friend of mine from HMS Diamond from when I was stationed in Chatham. His name was Ally Alright. Now Ally had been a Navy footballer, Navy boxer, brilliant darts player, play him at cards and you'd lose, was good looking and he had all the girls. I thought I knew all of Ally's talents but here in Casablanca, guess who was top of the bill doing Sinatra and Tony Bennett numbers, only Ally Alright.

The girls available were young, pretty and with lovely figures. Their hair was usually long and in a variety of colours. However, when bedtime came, their hair would just be tight kinks as their long blonde or ginger tresses would be placed on the bedpost. These girls were very tough and after being with one, if she saw you chatting up another night's entertainment, she would be liable to come over and knock your new conquest out. It was rumoured at that time that why the girls were willing was because they craved half- caste children and we certainly did our bit.

Chapter 10 – Cape Town & Durban during Apartheid

Calling at Cape Town in the late sixties, we docked at Simonstown which was a naval base a few train stops from the city itself. The very first time at Simonstown we were met with apartheid as soon as we got outside the dockyard gates. At this time, I was serving on H.MS Zulu and we had a lad on our messdeck who was black. His name was Esau but we nicknamed him Easy. He was very popular and liked by most. There were about six of us who had decided to go ashore together and this included Easy. As soon as we got outside the gates Easy was told by a police officer to get over the road on the black side. This at first seemed somehow comical but on reflection was very cruel. Here was Easy in a strange country and as soon as he's ashore loses the safety of his mates.

We went as sailors do into the very first pub available. Prior to this since leaving Singapore en route to Cape Town I had been on a health kick, giving away my tot and not smoking. On this day not only did I have my tot but also a few wets from friends I had been giving mine to. But up to now no cigarettes and I had intended to buy a pack as soon as I got ashore. Whilst in the first pub after setting down with our beers, a leading hand purchased a handful of cigars. Until now whenever I'd had a cigar such as at Christmas etc I'd want a fag in between puffs, but this one I really enjoyed and have smoked them for the past forty years.

All of the pubs we wandered into had "Whites Only" displayed with great clarity outside. Nearly all conversation with locals was political. It seemed the whites who were either Dutch settlers, white Africans or English didn't agree with each other and none of them liked the Blacks. Easy, however, didn't have to listen to all the crap as the "Blacks Only" bars were packed with people having a good time to lively music and he had a good run ashore.

On one Sunday morning three of us decided to take the train to Cape Town and to stop off at what looked like an interesting place called Fishoek on the way. Departing the station we soon realized we'd made a mistake as all the pubs were shut on Sundays. There was only one thing to do which was to go back to the station and get the next train to Cape Town. Back at the station we were the only ones there apart from a girl at the end of the platform who looked like a very pretty white girl with blonde hair. With nothing else to do until the next train's arrival, we decided to go and chat to the lone girl. "Please don't speak to me," she said when we were still a few feet from her. Asking what the reason was, she replied, "I'm black and I don't want locking up for talking to you." Here you had a girl whiter than us as we were tanned, not allowed to speak to us as she was black, which was absurd.

The beaches in Cape Town and Durban also were kept with great prejudice. All the great lengths of golden sand were clearly marked with "Whites Only" whereas the grey areas, where the sewage came out, were "Blacks Only".

Also at this time, there was a First World War hero, who in his later life was found to be black so he was stripped of his medals, although he'd lived as a white man all his life.

Being on HMS Zulu we treated Durban as our home town since Durban borders the Zulu territories. I was privileged to go and visit a Zulu school. We were met by the teachers who were all white and taken into a hall where a choir sang to us and I have never heard better singing. They even sang "The Zulu Warrior" which was forbidden. At dinner time we sat with some teachers on the top of a bank drinking ice cold coffee and eating a very tasty sausage with freshly cooked bread. The conversation was excellent and we learned that the children passed out with certificates higher than our GCE standards. Should a child fail, they would be sent back to the tribe and tied to a tree and beaten by everyone in the tribe. I later learned this to be completely true but the beatings were no more than a slight tap and the pass rates were so high – there were very few beatings. I also learned that their sense of time was non–committal. At the end of term they were all taken to the railway station from where their only train was at eleven in the morning. They would arrive at the station at nine o'clock where they would sit in groups of friends. When the train came in, only a few would get on. The rest were quite happy to wait twenty four hours for the next one. The following day would be the same so it could take a week before they all departed.

Durban Race Course was a place I loved to visit. It seemed, somehow, that you were transported back in time to the Victorian days and you were part of the wealthy. On one occasion I was ashore with my mate Nutty Slack when a rather large well- dressed young man came over and asked us if after the next race we would be kind enough to join a man whose name I can't remember for a drink. With this he pointed up to an old man who waved down at us. We agreed and after the race we went up to a very select bar. The old man was standing at the bar with a few friends. He seemed about eighty, was immaculately dressed and having introduced himself, asked our names. The moment we had a drink in our hands he decided to make a statement that he was ashamed to be British. Asking why, he replied that for years South Africa had shown us how to treat blacks and we'd taken no notice. He then went on about how we housed and fed them and what had any black man ever done for us. To this I quite simply replied, "Johnny Ghurkha". I then said to Nutty, "Let's get out of here," and not even finishing our drink, which was very unusual, we left. The strange thing was when they cheered their selections home, the jockeys were all black.

Durban was also home to "The Lady in White" who I saw on a few occasions. It was said that she'd sung in every British warship since the war. A Rolls Royce would take her to the end of the pier where, with a large microphone she'd sing Vera Lynn hits to the incoming vessel. No matter what the weather was doing, she would be there with white veils flowing in the wind, bellowing out "There'll be bluebirds over the white cliffs of Dover," or some such number. It certainly wasn't blackbirds.

She may not look much but she can't half cook

Chapter 11 – St Helena

There was a lad called Joss who was sailing on a frigate which was passing St Helena about one week ahead of us on HMS Ajax. Now St Helena is a small island in the South Atlantic and Joss hadn't been home for seven years so his ship was to drop him off and we were to pick him up seven days later. Although I didn't get to know Joss at this time, I later sailed with him on a Shell tanker and we became good friends.

On the day we stopped to pick him up we were granted shore leave. No taxis needed, we walked ashore into what seemed exactly like an English village. There was a schoolhouse, post office, village shop, pub and garage. We went to see what was their pride and joy – a collection of massive tortoises which Napoleon had given to them whilst he lived there in his exile years. A dance had been laid on for the evening in the schoolhouse and after our trek up Jacobs Ladder to see the giant tortoises; we quite looked forward to a few drinks and the evening's entertainment. Jacob's Ladder had 699 steps, so a thirst ensued.

Unfortunately for us St Helena had no airport and their only food and drink came in by boat, so catering for well over a hundred thirsty sailors was impossible and in less than two hours we had literally drunk them dry. So it was back on board for a very early night for most.

Apart from the shortage of alcohol this was a place to which I've always wanted to return. The people had been very friendly and the island had seemed so laid back and peaceful. The scenery was stunning, and although so far away it gave you the feeling of home from home.

Chapter 12 – Singers

When I first went to Singapore it was a right den of iniquity. For very little money you could partake in any vice known to mankind. The naval dockyard was huge and in the sixties would have more naval ships berthed than there would be in the whole Navy today. Just up from the dockyard was HMS Terror which was a great place to be based. There was a smaller messdeck berthing – about six. We were used to at least thirty, a large swimming pool, the best football field in the Far East and it was floodlit. The NAAFI bar was great. Like in Hong Kong you got sixteen pints for a pound. In the evenings the bar got packed. A lot of the sailors had dogs, mostly strays they'd befriended, some had monkeys and also there was the odd parrot. Very often a fight would break out and apart from the sailors, dogs, monkeys and even the parrots would get involved.

There was a huge fat Chinaman called P.Nut who collected your laundry. You would hear him every day going from one accommodation block to the next shouting out, "Left, Right, Left, Right, Dhobi, Dhobi, Left, Right, All Free, Pay Payday." P. Nut was quite a businessman as apart from a very busy laundry service, he also had a few bars in Sambawang village which was just outside the dockyard. He also was the man to ask when you would be sailing and where to.

He was never wrong and knew more than your captains.

In the dockyard itself was a Dockyard Club. This was the busiest drinking establishment I've ever been in. To get to the bar you could join a queue of a hundred. You never bothered to get a pint or two – you got a couple of buckets full – some even used a tin bath.

At least once a week we'd get a taxi into Singapore itself. You could pay a flat rate and have the cab to yourselves or get a "Pick Up". This was a lot cheaper as you picked up anybody who paid for the distance they'd travelled. So for instance if they went halfway then half the fare was payable by them. We'd usually get the taxi to stop at the Brick Club which was a combined Services club offering a good swimming pool and a fine bar. This was situated over the road from the world famous Raffles Hotel. It was at Raffles one night, having changed into civilian clothes in the Brick Club, where I had gone to see if I could espy Hayley Mills, the film star and daughter of John Mills, who had become a Sir. Sitting across from us was a table of what we called Rich Whites. This was a name we gave to anyone who had more money than us, which was virtually the rest of the white race. Anyway, this table of good people were being served their cocktails by a waiter whose backside was right in my view. What got into me, apart from the drink I'd consumed, I don't know, but I put my boot up his posterior causing the tray of drinks to saturate the good people he was serving. In no time at all I was ushered off the premises with a well- deserved life time ban. That was the closest I ever got to Hayley Mills.

Not far from Raffles was an assortment of bars. You could wander in and spy on a couple of shipmates in a dark corner, apparently enjoying a beer and a smoke with a look of glee on their faces. Then after a couple of minutes two girls would appear from under the table – these were "Wanky Wanky" bars.

Around ten o'clock at night you would make your way to Bugis Street. This was a long road with stalls, tables and chairs on both sides selling food, beer and gifts until daybreak. Hundreds of sailors, soldiers, airmen and tourists gathered there. This was also the place where "Kai Tois" came. They were mainly young men dressed like women and in fact the only way you could tell them apart was that the Kai Tois were better looking. There were many mistakes made with these and not all genuine. You also had young children of four or five who would play you noughts and crosses for a few dollars or even a few hundred. This was a simple game which you could never beat them at. Every now and again you might draw but this was the best you'd do.

There was a toilet which you entered at your peril. This had a flat roof where another form of entertainment took place – "The Dance of the Flaming Asrsehole". Sailors would climb on top, stick a few feet of toilet paper up their bums and set it alight. Where the toilet paper came from I don't know as certainly there wasn't ever any in the toilet.

On the way back we used to stop off at a stall in Nee Soon village for the best soup in the world – Heinz Tomato – and also get an egg banjo for breakfast later. This comprised an omelette made in a large wok. The beaten eggs would be thrown all around the top of the wok so it would cover the whole of it, then when rolled up you would have loads of layers. This would be put in a long soft roll, placed on a newspaper then wrapped with an elastic band to hold it together. When you came to eat it a few hours later, apart from eating it, you could also read it as the ink from the paper had penetrated the roll. They were delicious. I used to love the food from the stalls. A lot of people thought them to be unhygienic as it wasn't uncommon to see rats and there would be cockroaches everywhere, but to me they were very fine as you could see everything you wanted before and during cooking. Most meals were one dollar and you had eight dollars to the pound so happy days.

On one occasion in the early hours down Bugis Street, I met a young marine from our ship who was a nephew of Jimmy Savile. Sharing quite a few beers together we got quite friendly and he told me about letters he had from his uncle, pleading for young marines or sailors to write to him. When we got back on board ship he told me that if I wanted to I could go round to his mess later and he'd show me the letters. I was shocked on reading them, some of which had been pinned to the messdeck notice board and Mr Savile's intentions were quite plain. Later it became common knowledge throughout the fleet that Jimmy Savile was homosexual. Today with all the research going on into his devious past, I am amazed that his interests were also with young girls.

Walking past some of the shops in Singapore one afternoon, I couldn't believe what I had just seen, so I stopped and walked back to the window which had caught my attention. The window was covered in photos of assholes, half of which had bunches of grapes and other fruit- like beings protruding and the other half were normal. Looking up at the shop sign it was displayed that this was a piles doctor. The photos showed the before and after and it was a good job he was doing as well.

Considering all the vice there was available, which included opium dens, it was surprising there were no movie theatres showing porn. Instead what would happen in Sambawang village was that taxi drivers would approach you to take you to see blue movies. When three or four taxis were filled, you'd head off into a clearing in the jungle where a sheet would be hung from a tree and the camera placed on the top of the taxi. These films left nothing to the imagination and the taxi drivers knew that when the films were finished we would be looking for girls and they obviously knew where they could be found. One famous prostitute was Minnie No Nose – apparently the Japanese had cut off her nose during the war. Getting on in years and obviously no pin up, Minnie still made plenty of money keeping perverted young sailors happy.

Chapter 13 – The Bugler

At about eleven o'clock in the morning two Scottish friends called Nick Whelan and Jock Strachan and I wandered into the China Fleet Club in Hong Kong. The bar was empty apart from a soldier sitting on his own. He had his cap and a bugle on the table in front of him. As he looked lonely we did the proper thing and joined him. He was pleased with this as he said he was "pissed off" and had been playing his bugle at some memorial and it had taken hours.

The draft Tiger beer in the Fleet Club was fantastic; ice cold with slithers of ice that melted on your tongue. Sixteen dollars to the pound and a pint was one dollar – how could you beat that? Anyway, we did justice to the rate of exchange and the great beer, cheered our new friend up and settled into a good session. About five in the evening he fell asleep with his head on the table, so on our way out we decided to relieve him of his cap and bugle. On the way back to our ship HMS Ajax the bugle was our first fascination, but no way could any of us get a noise out of it, never mind a tune. We blew it, banged it, kicked it but silence remained. Fed up with our musical talent, the cap now became our focus of attention and an argument ensued over who was to wear it. Back on board, the bugle got its attention back. Everyone in our messdeck had a go and then it did its rounds of the ship; eventually it found a player who bought it back to our messdeck where we must have heard Reveille a hundred times before he was told to "shut the fuck up". The next day all hell broke loose as apparently the bugle was solid silver. It had been played in numerous famous battles. It was the Regimental Bugle and was insured for thousands of pounds. I was called to see my Divisional Officer who told me he knew the culprits, but if the bugle was intact and put in his cabin within the hour, that would be an end to the matter. The bugle was returned although it had more dents now than after all the great battles in which it had been played, but was intact. I later found out that the soldier had been picked up by the Red Caps, taken back to the Barracks and charged with improper dress (no cap) and the loss of the Regimental Bugle and received ninety days in detention. Sorry Mate!

Chapter 14 – DQs Detention Quarters

Portsmouth DQs was probably the hardest ordeal in the whole prison system. Should your crime be thought to have been too serious for a ship's punishment, DQs is where you'd end up. There were three time periods depending on your misdemeanour. The lightest being twenty- eight days, which had seven days remission, so twenty- one days you served. The next was forty- two days with fourteen days remission; for the most serious, ninety days with thirty days remission. Be good and you only served sixty. Losing your remission was very easy – one word or nod to someone not in authority and your remission was gone. Other crimes were numerous to keep you in the extra days.

From getting in the gates silence was observed unless spoken to by someone in authority. You doubled (ran) everywhere, one bowl of water a day to do everything – shave, clean teeth, wash, and drink. Your cell was small; your bunk was hard with only one coarse blanket. You also had a spittoon which had to be kept immaculate. Your day started with the assault course then carried on with an assault on life course. Your hair was shaved off on entry, food was crap, basic but adequate. Even if you only had twenty- one days you emerged lean and fit.

For the first seven days you didn't get a smoke, then on the eighth, spittoon in your left hand, you paraded in a circle to two patrolmen, the first of whom put a cigarette in your spittoon. You then took it out and placed it in your mouth where the second patrolman lit it. On the eighth day you never got your fag as your spittoon would be knocked to the floor "Filthy" but thereafter you got one. There was another snag with your smoke because after being lit you walked around in a circle having to stub it out in your spittoon on reaching the first patrolman. This was fine if there was a lot in, but if everyone had been behaving and there were only a few bad boys in, by the time you'd walked round a small circle you were stubbing out after only a few drags.

Should this sort of establishment be used in Civvy Street today, I'm convinced fortunes could be saved and you wouldn't have as many wanting a second dose.

Chapter 15 – Sexual and other Diseases

The night before arrival in any port in the world a message would be relayed by a tannoy system. Always strongly conveyed in these messages was not to go with the local girls. They would always be poxed up with every type of venereal disease – in fact your bits could fall off just by chatting them up. Red light districts and certain bars and streets would be strictly out of bounds. Of course, we took note of these as this would be where we would be heading.

The Royal Navy had a strange thing about sex. They'd take 300 young men to sea for a few weeks, homosexuality was taboo and if caught, apart from getting detention, you would be kicked out in disgrace. Yet when you got in port girls were put on the Not To Do List. At Ganges there were no toilet doors as bashing the bishop (wanking) was a crime. Unfortunately for the powers above we took no notice and, unfortunately for us, we paid the consequences. A few days on after leaving port the Doc would be busy curing our sick pricks. Along with the disgusting medicines came a thirty- day stoppage of leave and rum. The Americans had it worse than us as, if they contracted a venereal disease, they'd have to wait and pay to get it treated ashore because, if reported, they would get thrown out of the Services and back in America would become second class citizens. I do not understand

46

how they could hang on for treatment ashore as the pain "pissing razor blades" is what you feel.

Other diseases we were prone to were Malta Dog "shits" – you wouldn't have to be in Malta to catch this, it could be anywhere. Living so close together did not help. The most common explanation was "shitting through the eye of a needle".

Chinky Foot Rot was another disease most caught. It affected inbetween your toes and around your bollocks. It was very itchy and would become red raw and you would continually scratch both areas, spreading it further.

Crabs were a big problem as they spread like wildfire. Whilst serving on HMS Hampshire all of us stokers caught them. We were issued with sacks of some sort of powder and had to cover ourselves and our kit with it. It got everywhere and we were sweeping it up for weeks. Being so powdery, we all got coughs. The crabs disappeared and probably choked to death.

Scurvy was one time a very popular complaint. This was from where we got the nicknames Limeys, as lime juice was issued as a deterrent. The stuff we got certainly worked, and I never heard of one case of scurvy, as it would have killed anything, and you could feel your tooth enamel being eaten after one sip.

"Dhobi Dhobi Dhobi never goes ashore
Never has to muster at the Sick Bay door."

(Dhobi was your Chinese Laundryman)

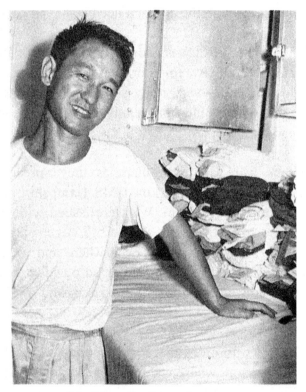

Mr Ling the Laundryman

Chapter 16 – Runs Ashore in London

Whilst stationed in Chatham, Kent, on the Duke of Edinburgh's old ship HMS Diamond we very often would get the train to London for a cheap day out. This would be achieved by paying the train fare, putting a ten bob note in your sock for emergencies; you then put a few coins in the pocket of your uniform and off you went. The best plan was for just two of you as three or more would seem greedy. On entering a pub you fumbled around to find the change to buy two halves of the cheapest bitter and in no time at all other customers, when purchasing their own drinks, would tell the barman to get those sailors a drink. Being rude to refuse, we instantly went onto pints of the best. Later in the day we'd request large whiskies or rum. If we were asked to join company and started to feel hungry, one of us would say, "I'm starving – fancy sharing a packet of crisps." Nine times out of ten we'd then be invited out for a meal. Never refusing, we'd do the restaurant justice and have the best of steaks. We had a lot to thank the sailor's uniform for.

On one occasion I got an early train and my mate Sheriff was to follow on a couple of hours later. When I got there with time to kill I decided to visit a bookmakers for a few small bets. Whilst I was studying where to put my shilling each way I felt a touch on my shoulder but thought nothing of it. About ten minutes later a man came up to me and gave me a five pound note, explaining that the horse that had just run and won was called Sailors Collar and he'd touched my collar for luck. On meeting Sheriff at the station I told him of my bit of fortune and we both decided that as "easy come", we would try our luck on one more horse and should it lose we'd just do our normal poverty routine. Back in the bookies we picked out a horse called Spring Cabbage and I put the whole fiver on. The horse duly won at one hundred to seven. Seventy pounds was a fortune and today we'd buy our own food and drinks, which we did in great abundance. In the evening we headed into Soho looking for girls. Seeing a club which looked to have what we were searching for, we paid the entrance fee and went up some stairs where we had to knock at a door. A shutter opened and closed and the door opened to display a low- lit room with a bar and a small dance floor. There were half a dozen girls and some smartly dressed hard looking men. On being served our very expensive drinks it was explained to us that to take a girl out you had to spend twenty pounds on drinks for them. This could be done in one hit or, if you wanted to talk for a while, you could buy two or three. The girls who came over were very attractive so we decided we'd just buy the one and take them out. We were then told we had to pay a returnable deposit of five pounds per girl and this was to make sure we brought them back safely. Ready to go, we were then told to wait over the road by a butcher's shop and as soon as the girls' reliefs came they would come out to us. Everything seemed correct and sensible. We waited outside the butcher's shop for about half an hour when it started to rain heavily. Getting fed up I decided to go back and find out what was happening. Having been told they were on their way we went back and waited another half an hour. We could now see we were being conned so decided to go and get our money back. This time we were met by the heavies who quite plainly told us to fuck off. At the top of the stairs Sheriff stopped me from taking a pop at the heavy brigade and at the bottom of the stairs I stopped Sheriff from setting light to the place. Apart from the most expensive beer in the world, I'd paid fifty pounds for nothing.

Chapter 17 – Dirty Dicks

My main station to and from Norfolk was Liverpool Street. Over the road is a pub called Dirty Dicks which has a bar at street level and one below. Now Dirty Dick was a chap in some distant past who got fed up with cleaning himself and his establishment and swore at one uncertain time never to clean either again until the day he died. Apparently he sewed himself into his clothes and kept to his word.

Now at the time I was a frequent visitor. The downstairs bar kept to the theme with mummified dead cats and dogs hanging from the ceiling, and walls covered by autographed fag packets, photos or whatever you could find to pin up. The floor was inch deep in sawdust.

It was here that I had two very unusual happenings of which I will tell. The first, I was on leave from the Merchant Navy and about eleven o'clock one weekday morning I wandered down the steps to the bar to get my first pint of the day. Sitting at the bar was a short thickset fellow in his mid-sixties with a glass of barley wine. There being no-one else in the bar I pulled up a stool and sat down. "Hello mate, what's your name? I'm known as the Big Hitter," was how the stranger introduced himself. Round for round we went, me and the Big Hitter, who had removed his cap to show a sweating bald pate. The place was filling up now with dinnertime trade, office workers and tourists and by the jukebox a group of lads from a building site. The Big Hitter was looking anxious now and casting his eyes from person to person. All of a sudden his eyes must have met with one of the builders and up he shot, placing his cap back on his head, and downing the last of his barley wine, he shot across to the jukebox area, hitting the unfortunate builder with a punch equal to Marciano's KO of Jersey Joe. The last I ever saw of the Big Hitter was of him scarpering up the stairs giving a goodbye wave to me as he went.

On another occasion on a dinner time I wandered down the steps where at the bottom was a large barrel with smaller barrels surrounding, forming table and chairs. I noticed a lone figure sitting on one of the barrels, drinking a pint. Going to the bar to get my refreshment I noticed the place to be packed, so after getting my pint I thought I'd join the lone fellow at the bottom of the steps. Asking if he'd mind if I joined him, I sat on one of the barrels. "Do you know it's a fact," he said in a Dublin brogue, "you can't get drunk sitting on a barrel?" After quite a few rounds and good conversation my new- found friend decided to leave, only after about three steps he fell back landing heavily on his arse. In my drunken stupor I managed to pick him up and placed him once again on his barrel where he immediately passed into a drunken slumber. So without further conversation possible I decided to leave, giving him a good shake on my way and having said my goodbyes, reminded him that you can't get drunk sitting on a barrel.

Chapter 18 – The Unforgettable Aussie Gaye

I first met Aussie at Heathrow Airport when like myself and a few others he was flying out to join a Shell tanker, He was in his sixties, smoking a pipe and dressed in blazer, shorts, shiny black shoes and no socks. His white hair was full and cut in a rather spiky crew cut. He also had the longest eyebrows I'd ever seen. Aussie wasn't Australian as his name suggested. He was from Dock Street in London. His name came about as years before he had adopted Australia himself to become his homeland when on leave. While we used to spend six months on a ship, Aussie would do two years in order to build up his leave up to about six months. When he left a ship he would get a flight to Australia where he would charter a plane into the outback. He bought a horse, gun and cooking pots and enough food for the horse to carry. In his own words, he then would ride into the outback and make camp. "Soon as I shit up the area I moved on." It was on one of these expeditions when Aussie found the only family he ever had. The rainy season had started and in slippery conditions the horse fell and broke its leg so it had to be put down. Aussie then walked for days, soaking wet and with very little food left and his legs cut to bits by the rapidly growing grass, he started to get covered in boils and thought his end was nigh. Out of nowhere an Aborigine boy appeared and helped Aussie onto his own horse, then took him back to his family's meagre shack where they cared for him until he had fully recovered. They then became his family.

He once built a fence a hundred miles long and each post had to be dug out by hand. This task was done with the help of a mate and his son.

The best of Aussie's tales was when he was in an Australian regiment during the war. In the midst of a very fierce battle, the Germans stopped firing. Then somebody shouted across, "What the fuck's up with you guys?. The reply came, "We're out of ammo." They then called back, "Well for fuck's sake have some of ours," which they did and the battle continued.

His remedies for health were completely unique; not being able to shit he went to the Chief Steward who told him to eat bran. So Aussie had a whole large box every day for breakfast, then he got piles so the steward told him to stop shitting. The answer to this was he ate a box of bran every day and only shat on Sundays when he had a day off. If he was watch keeping he didn't shit for a month. It was best to keep away from his cabin at this time.

If he felt crook (ill) he had his hair cut; for anything else like cuts or knocks he'd go to the steward for a tot of rum. For all his strange quirks he was very fit and had a very muscular body. As a young man on a ship's visit to the Argentines he'd sparred with none other than Jack Dempsey.

Our dining room was also used for film shows, and it also had a fridge which was used for snacks. Aussie would use it for his beer and also enquired whether or not we had a Talking Picture (he'd not seen a film since talkies started and reckoned he couldn't understand what was going on with all the yapping). He'd learnt not to come in during a film as he'd always walk in front of the camera and when we all could see a spiky haired silhouette disturbing the film, we'd shout out, "Get your fucking head down." Years later when we had videos he'd still duck down when he came in for his beer. Somebody once asked Aussie about a film John Wayne was in. "Who's John Wayne mate?" he replied. The last time I sailed with Aussie he was in his seventies and learning Chinese.

Chapter 19 – Japan

I consider myself lucky to have visited Japan on a few occasions whilst serving in both the Royal and Merchant Navies. Japan was strange in that although the people seemed to have a very similar lifestyle to our own, as they liked a drink, to smoke, bet and sport, it was the hardest place I'd been to be understood.

Dining was complete luck as in those days nothing was written in English. The easiest way to get any food was to go to the bar and, when you had attention, point to your mouth and then to a diner's plate, and say, "That will do for me." You'd obviously picked a plate of food to point at which looked good, but what you'd get was a different matter. The very first time I'd done the pointing game a plate of rice was put by what I thought was an ornamental fish tank. Next thing a small net was plunged into the tank scooping up half a dozen different coloured fish, which in seconds flat were hacked into a hundred bits and stirred into the rice. There was no way I would eat that so settled for just rice and Soya sauce.

Moji was a Japanese naval town where we were made exceptionally welcome. There was a bar we found which was very popular with young locals of our age. It had a jukebox and there was no problem with dining as there was a P- nut machine. Continually playing on the jukebox were The Beatles, which they loved, but when you mentioned The Rolling Stones, they'd never heard of them. So the next night we took them some Rolling Stones singles which the landlord kindly put on the jukebox. On hearing them, they went down a bomb so I like to think I introduced The Rolling Stones to Japan.

Also on this night there were signs advertising a five thousand yen reward for the thief who'd taken our means of nourishment – the P- nut machine. In those days the rate of exchange was one thousand yen to the pound, so this was a good reward.

There were three of us ashore together and after a few drinks we started to fancy getting a prostitute each for the night. We had a large problem with this, though, as only one of us could afford one and it wasn't me. Right in front of us was the answer. Flip a coin and the winner reports the other for the theft of the P- nut machine, collect his reward and happy days. The coin was tossed by our mate who already had the money and I was the lucky winner. On grassing up my mate I was taken aback by not instantly getting my ill-gotten gains, but not long after the local Police came in and escorted the loser away. After this I was paid my reward. Only spending one night in jail, my mate was let out with no charge – after all he hadn't nicked it anyway. As for me, I had my night of pleasure with many thanks to the P- nut machine.

When you went with a girl in Japan they were very attentive to cleanliness. The first thing they'd do was shower you using fragrant smelling soap, then you would be bathed in a bath which was at floor level and about a metre square. It was just deep enough that your protruding head and neck were above the very hot water. When they were satisfied you were clean enough, you would be dried by hot towels and given a very relaxing massage. This would be followed by a glass of warm saki. I think there were double meanings for all the pampering as after the dirty deed was done, you slept like a baby, which ensured them a good night's sleep too.

The Police, although always smiling, were a little gun happy. We'd gone ashore in Yokahama and we were looking for a taxi into Tokyo. Trying to hail one down was impossible as they were passing us doing what looked like ninety miles an hour. On a traffic island in the middle of the road was a policeman who must have spotted us trying to stop a cab. "Taxi," he called to us, which must have been the only word we had in common. We nodded back in agreement. With this he drew his pistol, put his whistle in his mouth and blew. Like magic a taxi screamed to a halt instantly. Thanking him, we boarded the taxi thinking whatever would have happened if he hadn't have stopped. On another occasion whilst walking down a busy street in Tokyo, a young man sprinted past us and was shot dead by a smiling policeman who was in chase.

60

There were lots of bars where we couldn't get served. The reason being that if they served us there wouldn't be room for their regulars as each bar could only hold about a dozen people. Walking into one of these bars one afternoon, the barman said in very good English, "Come in boys. I'll buy you a drink." He was a man in his forties and when we'd settled on high stools around the bar, he explained that he'd been a young man on the Burma railroad, working as a guard. This had been his first chance since those days to apologize for his part in what he said disgusted him 'til this day. He seemed genuinely sorry and we told him that he was only doing his duty and shook his hand. We spent about two hours in this bar and didn't spend a penny. Before leaving we were given a very fiery spirit and on departing, with tears in his eyes, he hugged each and every one of us. I am sure this man was sincere and he'd given us a very enjoyable afternoon.

Kiri was another coastal town where I enjoyed a new experience – the beer garden. These days, especially with the smoking ban, beer gardens are very popular in England, but in the sixties I hadn't heard of one – tables and chairs outside maybe. We'd got taxis for a short distance into the Japanese countryside where this beer garden was. Surrounding a very oriental- type building were round tables with a hole in the middle and bench- type seating. It was very cold and started to snow, which made us think that this might not be the smartest of ideas. There were ten of us and we managed to all get around one table. Parasols were put over us, which kept a lot of the snow off us, and placed in the hole in the middle of the table was a canister of hot coals. It wasn't long before we started to heat up and the beer was going down well. After about half an hour a large metal plate was placed over the hole. Oil was brought and bowls of raw meats – chicken, pork and something which resembled beef. There were also prawns and fish and a very large bowl of rice. Each one of us was then given a bowl and chopsticks. We then cooked whatever we wanted ourselves to our own perfection. It was one of the finest meals I have ever had. Drinking ten pints of beer each, the final bill was ten thousand yen – only a pound each with the food being free. However, there was a snag. Throughout the time there we all had to keep moving our legs about as the heat from the fire got unbearable and the next day, on inspection of our bell bottoms, most were singed beyond repair.

The ship at Moji, Japan

Chapter 20 – Baccy

At seven shillings for 600 fags there were very few non smokers. I mean in today's money that's thirty-five pence – the price of one fag. You had a choice of tipped or plain, pipe or hand rolling baccy.

The cigarettes were called blue liners as each one had a blue line down it. They were boxed in twenties in a white carton with a blue line down the centre with an R on the left and an N on the right. Prior to joining the Navy, although most of my mates smoked, I didn't. Whilst at Ganges every break was announced, "Ten minutes for a smoke," and you'd watch your mess mates drag away seeming to get great pleasure and relaxation. I had to join this. At first, all they did was make me cough and go heady but I persevered, practising in the toilets until I mastered the act. Smoking on board ships in those days must have been very unhealthy. Your messdecks were small and you could have forty ratings smoking away with no portholes for fresh air. On one occasion, a P.T.I (physical training instructor) on our messdeck decided to give up. He decided to take away his cravings by eating a handful of peanuts. After a few weeks his previously athletic body started to gain fat, so not happy with this he reverted back to smoking. The only trouble was he couldn't give up the peanuts either so he was hooked on both.

Cigarettes were also stowed in lifeboats which today they are not, and I think this ruling should be reversed. My reasoning for this is that lifeboats can only carry limited food and smoking takes away hunger pangs. Lester Piggott, the best jockey that ever lived, kept his weight down over a long career by smoking large cigars. Also, for those unlucky enough to have suffered life in a lifeboat, having a cigarette two or three times a day became the highlight of the day and also relaxed the tension.

Chapter 21 – Freetown

Whilst on Beira patrol when serving on HMS Zulu it was decided to give us a day's leave in Freetown. Beira patrol was tedious with little to break the monotony apart from sporting matches with other ships. The prize was to win a bucket which was named the Beira Bucket. Although these competitions helped to break the boredom, a run ashore was what was needed.

We had our normal lecture about how poxed up the local girls were and how dangerous Freetown was, which at the time it was. So we decided to get one of the buses that had been provided to go to a local beach. On arrival at the beach, we unloaded our cases of Tennants and settled in different groups. The beach was clean and picturesque with palm trees and the sea was deep blue. It was very hot, around a hundred degrees, so frequent dips in the sea were essential On one of the many times I'd been in to cool off, I decided to go out a bit further, but when trying to swim back, I found myself drifting further down the coast instead of back to where we'd set up camp. Being a strong swimmer I was not alarmed and headed to a part of the beach about half a mile from where I'd wanted to be. As soon as it was shallow enough I started to scramble out but my feet kept sliding back into the oily mud which was nearly up to my knees before I could make further progress. The stink was unbearable. It took me half an hour before I was on clean sand. I was covered in this oily black crap which on closer inspection was all moving like minute maggots. Talking to some of the locals later I discovered that the point I'd swam into was where the fishing boats had landed up until the area had got so bad they were forced to move. I had obviously waded through years of rotted fish guts. On arrival back at where we'd set up camp my mates begged me to get back in the sea and clean off as, apart from the stink, I'd attracted every fly on the planet.

When the beer was all gone we decided to get a taxi to a bar. It was in this bar where the flies appeared again. They must have been homing flies because they were certainly attracted to me. I probably still stunk from fish gut beach. The clientele of our new- found bar were all casualties of the troubles. I didn't see one complete person. Over from our table was a fellow with no legs and only one arm, and this was in a sling. His mate who was feeding him his beer only had one leg and seemed to be blind. We had to cover our beers with years- old beer mats because of the fly situation and when a dog appeared with bald patches and pus-filled boil- like bumps; I decided to get a taxi back to the ship for a long overdue shower.

Chapter 22 – Aden

We called in at Aden on the way back from the Far East, where on HMS Hampshire we'd been involved in the Borneo War. It was Aden, however, where I was in the most dangerous situation. We were told on board ship that when ashore we should not go around in groups of any more than threes, the reason being that this was a smaller target for the insurgents.

The first street we came upon had a few bars, the first of which I and two mates entered. Inside were two sailors and three soldiers and the bar was a bit quiet as there was no jukebox, so I suggested wandering a bit further. The second bar also had no jukebox and was completely empty. On entering the third, not only was there a jukebox but it sold English beer "Watneys Red Barrel" and being quite lively, we decided to settle here. We ordered three pints of Red Barrel, which was the first English beer we'd tasted for nine months. Within seconds of taking my first sip there was an explosion outside, which sounded no more than a burst tyre. In no time at all Army Military Police (Red Caps) rushed into the bar, ordering everybody to get out and go over the road. Trying to down more of our long- awaited English beer, our glasses were smashed out of hands with truncheons and we were told again, this time with real urgency, to get the fuck over the road. On arrival at the other side of the road we could plainly see the first bar which had no jukebox had been blown up. Later we heard a grenade had been thrown in and all inside were killed.

We were picked up by an Army bus and escorted to a NAAFI in an Army camp where we were made extremely welcome. For years after I always looked for bars with a jukebox.

There was also another fatal incident of a different type this week. A young electrician on his lunch break decided to go sunbathing on the upper deck. He apparently fell asleep and sustained third degree burns from which he died later that day. I knew this lad well but it was especially bad for the two I'd been ashore with as they were good friends and messmates of his.

Chapter 23 – Shot at, Locked up, Stripped, Merry Christmas

On my first ship in the Merchant Navy, SS Methane Progress, we used to carry methane gas from Arzu in Algeria to Canvey Island in Essex on a ten- day return trip. Algeria was in conflict at this time and going ashore in Arzu was not pleasant. You would be searched at the gate going out and again on entry. Virtually everything you needed for a run ashore was banned; fags, lighter, money etc. We got round this by putting money in our sock. There were only a few bars, Big Tits being the most popular. It was in this bar that should you manage to smuggle ashore Oxo cubes or Magi, the lads working out there on construction from John Browns would get you pissed for nothing. There was a strict curfew and the Army and Police were everywhere, but they didn't seem to bother much about us.

Just outside the dockyard gates was the start of a range of hills, which for some reason fascinated me and I decided that the next time in Arzu I'd climb up and see what was what. The opportunity came on Boxing Day in 1972. I'd talked the deck boy and deck storekeeper in to coming on this adventure with me. We set off at around eleven o'clock and it was a lovely sunny day. Climbing to the top of the first hill we could see that a couple of miles down to the left there was a village and Arzu was then a few miles further on. We decided to walk along the tops of the hills then down to the village for a coffee and then to go along to Arzu for a couple of pints in Big Tits before getting a taxi back to the ship. After about a mile of walking, to our right about half a mile away we could see a circle of men "daisy chain I joked". As we were coming to a ridge overlooking the village there was a pillbox and from the top a soldier waved at us and shouted. Not understanding him we waved back, wishing him a "Merry Christmas". Starting down the hill towards the village, all of a sudden we could hear thudding into the hillside. "Get to the top of that ridge quick," I said, and we did so only to find when we got there that we were met by soldiers with bayonets fixed. We were pushed and prodded down the hill where the village turned out to be an Army camp. In the camp we were put up against a wall facing it with our arms up, but leaning. The deck storekeeper was very distraught – he was only young and not long married with a baby son. The deckboy was also frightened and sweated profusely. After about an hour an officer came over dangling his rifle in the dirt, I haven't a clue what he was on about but to me it seemed like continuous swearing. About an hour after he had left, four jeeps and an open- backed lorry with about twenty soldiers came over. We were bundled into the lorry with soldiers in front and at the back of us, two jeeps ahead and two behind us. We left the camp and headed into the desert. Trying to comfort the other two I honestly thought we were going to be shot. After what seemed like an eternity you could see buildings and as we got closer you could see we were heading for Arzu.

In Arzu, we were taken to the Police Station and as we were escorted in I spotted a man who had joined the ship called McClintoch. He was in his sixties and had spent the last thirty years on Liverpool buses. I was later to sail with his grandson Chris McClintoch. I called out to him and told him to go back and tell the old man (Captain).

In the Police Station, we were put in individual cells alongside each other, stripped of our clothing and this was taken away. After about an hour I heard one cell being opened and then closed again. Half an hour later and this was repeated in the other cell. A further half an hour later and it was my turn. Completely naked, I was marched past criminals and police to a large office where I had to stand at a massive desk. Sitting at the other side of this in what looked like a throne was the most decorated man I'd ever seen. He must have won every battle since Waterloo. I was told that I was to be questioned and should he think that I was lying, I would be taken away and await trial, which could be up to four years away. He also told me he had been trained at Sandhurst, as if that would change my plight. Apparently we were being considered spies. Thank God we didn't have a camera as obviously we would have taken photos of the circle of men, our friend in the pillbox and the village which was really an Army camp. I was questioned for at least an hour. The fact that I'd served in the Royal Navy didn't help and being put back in my cell I wasn't happy. After what seemed like an eternity we were given our clothes back and were handed over to the British Consul who, after shaking hands, got us a taxi back to the ship. I wanted to stop off at Big Tits to celebrate but my two friends just wanted to get back. The following day I was called up to see the Captain and had to explain what had happened. "Fuck that," he said, "I'm stopping all leave in Arzu forever," and so he did.

Chapter 24 – A Run Ashore that went Wrong

Whilst stationed at Rosyth on HMS Zulu, as we were getting bored with the local drinking establishments so we decided to have a coach trip out. A Leading Stoker took it upon himself to write to a dozen venues asking for their co-operation in entertaining thirty- two sailors on a Thursday at a designated time. The reason for a Thursday was we got paid on alternate Thursdays. He requested an extention as all drinking places in Scotland in those days closed at ten o'clock. Our other requests were for food, a darts match and possibly the presence of a few of the local girls. We got one reply which was from the Queen Hotel in Hawick. With no choice we opted for this venue and arrangements were made.

The day finally came and off we went. After stopping off on our way for a couple of pints, we arrived at the Queens Hotel about five in the evening. On entry we went into the Public bar but had noticed a Lounge bar with a small dance floor. Apart from us both bars were empty. The barman looked shocked as we went in as apparently nobody had told him we were coming. After an hour or so we were starting to feel peckish and with the darts match closing in, thought it about time to eat. Enquiring about the menu, our barman informed us there was no chef as nobody had booked, but said he'd sell us some crisps. Not happy with crisps, we sent someone out to get some pasties. On his return he'd bought scotch pies as there were no pasties. Now a scotch pie in Scotland is a way of disposing of grease and fat which they disguise in rather delightful pastry. So we filled the ashtrays with the filling and ate the pastry.

The darts match was getting closer so we started to practice but there was still no sign of any opposition. When questioned about their darts team the barman said, "I've never seen one but nobody tells me nothing." So now we had no meals and no darts match and there was no sign of any girls. In fact, there were still no locals at all so we got together half a dozen lads with enough good looks and charm and sent them out to get some local talent. After about an hour they returned from their mission, having failed. In fact, one lad had a bad scratch on his face from a girl who'd told him to "Fuck off to Glasgow if you want a prossie". God knows what chat up line he'd used.

Fed up with things now, some of us moved to the Lounge bar for a change of scenery and to make the best of a bad job. At ten o'clock on the dot the shutters came down. "We've got an extention," we told the barman who was the same one from the Public bar. "No one's told me about an extention," he said. Asking to see the management we were told, "They've gone out." Probably for a game of darts and something to eat we thought. The barman then decided we could buy carry- outs so in our group we purchased more booze. Me, Nutty Slack and a couple more bought a bottle of Scotch and twelve cans of Tennants.

The bus driver had been called and was waiting outside the front door. Unfortunately, so was the Law, who refused to let us out of the building and on to the bus with our carry- outs. An argument started and two of our lads were taken away and locked up. Back to the bar we went, asking the barman to buy back our booze. To go along with the rest of the evening we were refused. Our answer to this was we went into the toilets, slurped down whatever we could and threw the rest all over the place. When we left the toilets looked like a scene from Titanic.

When the bus pulled out we decided to lynch the Leading Stoker who'd organized the trip, and also a lad called Laidlaw who had the misfortune to come from Hawick. Our plan was put on hold when some genius decided to ask the driver to stop at a chippy. Starving, we all agreed and started to cheer up.

A few miles along in a small town the driver pulled up at a backstreet chippy. In we piled the thirty of us left and formed a reasonable queue. There were two cooks frying away with gusto. By the counter was a stack of newspapers to wrap your delicacies. Me and Nutty were at the rear of the queue so Nutty went and grabbed a couple of sheets of newspaper with the idea of passing some time making paper aeroplanes. On his first attempt he made a brilliant plane which resembled Concorde. Deciding on a test flight he launched it down the queue with the idea of twatting a comrade behind the ear. Unfortunately, the plane had its own ideas and did a brilliant turn, hitting a cook who was frying the chips instead. It then crashlanded into the chip pan. In no gentlemanly fashion we were all told to leave this frying establishment. Back on the bus, we had now had enough and reverted to Plan A with our plot to lynch Laidlaw and the organiser.

The author (sitting, far right) with Nutty Slack (wearing glasses)

Chapter 25 – Guinea Pig

On leaving HMS Ajax I was drafted to A.M.E.E Haslar, which as Haslar was a Naval Hospital in Gosport, I thought I would be looking after the boilers or some such thing. On arrival at the hospital nobody had heard of me and I certainly wasn't drafted there. After a few phone calls I was sent to HMS Dolphin, a base for submariners, which was just up the road. Nobody had heard of me there either and I was told to go back to the hospital. Back at the hospital I managed to baffle a few more people until a civvy who I took to be a gardener pointed to the end of the road and said, "Turn left there."

At the end of the road I turned left into a tarmac lane where after a couple of hundred yards was a gatehouse. The civilian on the gate pointed to some buildings in the distance. On letting me through, he told me it was an experimental station. As I walked towards the buildings I had terrible thoughts about the experiments they would conduct on me. I imagined being put in a cage and injected with lethal diseases for a team of boffins to try and cure.

On arrival at the buildings, I was directed to a bungalow by a civvy. Here I found out there were six ratings, me included, a chief stoker and an officer who only appeared fortnightly on pay days. Our sole duty was to raise a flag in the morning and take it down in the evening. We came under Victory Barracks but lived in HMS Dolphin which was very handy because we were virtually undetectable.

Our days were taken up by playing cards or having a kick around. As I intended trying for Field Gun, I started to get fit by doing a lot of running and sneaking off to the gym in Dolphin to do weights. We even got out of the task of pulling the flag down at night by bribing a civvy with fags to do it for us. I never did find out what experiments were taking place. I certainly never saw any headless sailors or three- titted jenny Wrens and I stayed there for seven months until I went in Field Gun.

Chapter 26 – Young and Old

Whilst serving on HMS Zulu, at one time I was the oldest on the messdeck. There were thirty- two of us and I was only twenty- four years old. We then had a Leading Hand join us who was thirty- five; this was ancient to us so we looked after our senior citizen well. Should the poor chap nod off, somebody would soon be there to give him a shake, making sure he was still alive.

The Royal Navy was manned in general by young men. However, it wasn't uncommon in the Merchant Navy to sail with men in their sixties and seventies. I have written earlier about Aussie Gaye, but another great character I sailed with was a man from the Orkney Islands called Kenny Ross. Kenny was around seventy and lived on the sea. Even on his leaves he was out all day on a fishing boat. At one time in his life, he'd spent seven years on a whaler.

Ali Said was another old timer I had the privilege to sail with a few times. Ali who was an Arab from the Yemen was married to an Irish woman and they lived in Hull with their sixteen children, half of whom he couldn't even remember their names. He had been at sea all his life and as a seaman he was useless, not even being able to tie a knot. But I am really pleased to have known him. His lack of seamanship was made up for by the fact it was great just to have him around. Whether his family thought the same was another matter. He had me in stitches when he told me about the time he'd arrived on leave around the fifth of November and the kids had put his best suit on the Guy.

Horse Tilsley like me was ex- Royal Navy and I sailed with him twice in Shell tankers. Horse was in his late fifties and a very heavy smoker and drinker. For leaves he would only last three or four days out of his six weeks. He would get a room in a pub, then himself and the pub's customers would drink his six months' wages away. With the extra treat of a prostitute, after three or four days he would be skint and phoned Shell to go back to sea. Horse had served with the Royal Navy in Kenya during the Mau Mau troubles in the nineteen fifties and unfortunately was very racist.

To be woken up in the Merchant Navy you were either phoned or given a shake, which meant a "watchkeeper" would enter your cabin and call you, or if in a deep sleep shake you. I was in my cabin one morning waiting to go to breakfast when I could hear a massive argument from Horse's cabin which was next door. Going to see what the problem was there was Horse at his door, naked, arguing with a black lad who had come to give him a shake. After defusing the situation I asked Horse what his problem had been. His answer being he'd been woken up and when he looked up, had thought it was the Mau Mau leaning over him so he went for his gun. I told him it was a lot of years since he had anything to do with guns, and that the watchkeeper was a good lad. Horse apologised to the lad, but true to his spirit would then take pot shots with his fingers at him, and this was taken in good spirits as he would get fired back on by imaginary arrows.

Chapter 27 – Bahrein

On leaving Field Gun I was drafted to HMS. Zulu and flew out to join it in Bahrein. When the plane doors opened the heat of the day moved in like an unstoppable force, and in seconds flat from being cool in the air conditioning you were saturated in sweat. So this was what it was like in the Persian Gulf, bloody hot.

The ship was berthed on a jetty a short walk from an army camp and the naval base. The army camp had a swimming pool which for some reason was built on stilts. We used the pool a lot but after a while they tested the water and found it to contain an abnormal amount of piss; being sailors we obviously were the culprits and got banned. This didn't stop us though as it was quite easy to break into, so we just changed our times and had many a midnight swim. This was also very handy as we'd be full of beer and there were no toilets on the way back to the ship.

Our bar in the naval base had no air conditioning so was very hot, the only way to cool down being to drink vast amounts of beer which we did. The bar in the army camp did have air con; on occasions we would go there for a change, but to us it seemed too cold, and you couldn't get quite the thirst.

One afternoon we went ashore to our bar to celebrate a young lad from our messdeck's eighteenth birthday. He came from Birmingham and his surname sounded Polish so we called him "Joe the Pole", although as far as we knew there was no Polish blood in him. Being Joe the Pole to us we clubbed together and bought him a fitting birthday gift which was a pint of vodka. Wishing him a happy birthday we clapped as he downed it in one. He seemed quite fine for a while, then he wandered off and sat down with an American who was with his wife. After about twenty minutes the American came over and said, "Come and get your buddy he's pissed himself." We laid Joe out on some grass and carried on drinking until the arrival of the ship's patrol. Seeing Joe flaked out on the grass they tried to wake him, but failing in their mission they called for a jeep to get him back on board. Not wanting to get him in trouble I quickly devised a plan to steal him. The idea was to divert the patrolman's attention and put Joe over a hedge until we were ready to go back on board. Luckily for me the jeep arrived before my plan could be put to use, as on arrival back on board, inspected by the doc he was rushed into hospital to have his stomach pumped out. Had I have stolen him I easily could have killed him.

It was in the same bar where I got in big trouble the night before I was to fly home for discharge. I was suffering from another type of discharge which I had obtained from a very nice girl in Banda Abbas, Persia so I was on thirty days stoppage of leave. Being my last night I decided to break ship for a final run ashore with my mates. There were about a dozen of us sitting around a table drinking away, and the empty glasses were stacking up in the middle of the table. There were three lads off a minesweeper playing darts, and one of my mates who was eating a plate of chips turned his chair round to watch them. Seeing his chips without asking they decided to help themselves, but taking umbrage an argument started. Knocking the first one out, I then got stuck into the second, the third then jumped on my back, but pulling him over he landed back first on the centre of our table where the glasses were piled high. The naval patrol were quick to arrive so we scarpered and made our way to the army camp. So I could keep my head down we purchased two cases of lager and found a quiet spot in the sand to finish the night off. On arrival back on board I was arrested and placed on captain's report for the following day. The day I was meant to be flying home.

When called to the captain's table I was surprised to see the three lads from the minesweeper and it didn't look good – one was on crutches, another was heavily bandaged from landing on the glasses, and all were badly bruised. What I didn't know, but the captain did, was that the same three had bullied two junior seamen earlier in the week. The captain was like Perry Mason and tore them apart. I got off scot-free, even for breaking ship so was on my way home for discharge.